Table

Introduction

If you are one of those people who love doing DIY projects, then this is exactly what you are looking for. Making scented candles are a natural and fantastic DIY project that you can make at home and enjoy doing it!!!

Making scented candles is the best thing ever because you actually get to try and make your own scents and decorate your candles to make them look expensive which make them a fabulous gift idea that will please anyone to have it. The second best thing about this project is the fact that the scent that you use you in your candles is from essential oils which make them so healthy and chemical free, so you don't have to worry about any chemical product at all.

You can play with the scents try every time a new set of essentials that will leave your house smelling amazing not to mention that you can make your candles in various shapes and colors, add to them pebbles and roses. It is an incredible chance for you to sooth your senses with you favorite scents and express you at the same time by freeing the artist in you.

Many people think that making candles at home is so expensive and will leave you with a huge mess when you are done which is not to true at all. The products used in these recipes are not used at all, and once you make your fist set of candles, you will be left out with so many products that you can use all over again for several times. When it comes to cleaning the wax, a simple damp cloth will do the trick for you and you will end up with a mess free working place!!!

So let the inner artist in you out and let us discover together where your talent will take you!!

• Amazing Vanilla Sanctuary Candle

Ingredients:

- 3 drops of vanilla essential oil
- 1 drop of sandalwood essential oil
- Mold sealer
- Mold release
- Double boiler
- Metal Pouring Pot
- Kitchen scale
- Mold-blend wax
- Thermometer
- Small tin container
- Mold: round pillar
- Metal skewer
- Primed wick, square braided
- Scissors

Directions:

1. Melt the wax in a double broiler then using a mold release; coat slightly the inside of candle mold.
2. Cut the wick to the appropriate length and thread it into the hole in the bottom of the mold and secure it.
3. Pour the melted wax in a metal pouring pot and stir into it right away the vanilla and sandalwood essential oils then fill 90 % of the mold with it and pour the excess wax into a tin container.
4. Allow the wax to sit then re-melt the excess wax and fill with it the indentation before leaving it to sit again.

5. Tip the mold upside down to remove the candle then trim the excess wick from the top and bottom of the candle before using it and enjoy.

The Best Embedded Lemony Lavender Candle

Ingredients:

- 2 drops of lemon essential oil
- 2 drops of lavender essential oil
- 1 drop of sage essential oil
- Metal Spoon
- 1 unscented pillar candle
- Mold sealer
- Mold release
- Double boiler
- Metal Pouring Pot
- Kitchen scale
- Mold-blend wax
- Thermometer
- Small tin container
- Mold: round pillar
- Primed wick, square braided
- Pebbles or Glass marbles

Directions:

1. Melt the wax in a double broiler then using a mold release; coat slightly the inside of candle mold.
2. Mix half the essential oils and set them aside.
3. Lighten the pillar candle and let it burn until a pool of wax gather on top of it then turn it off and make deep small on its top.
4. Pour the drops of the mixed oils into the holes then place the candle in the center of the mold and drop the pebbles of marbles in it until half of the mold is full.
5. Pour the melted wax in a metal pouring pot and stir into it right away the sage with lemon and lavender essential oils then fill 90 % of the mold with it and pour the excess wax into a tin container.

6. Allow the wax to sit then re-melt the excess wax and fill with it the mold before leaving it to sit again, while making sure not to pour it on the pillar candle.
7. Tip the mold upside down to remove the candle then use it and enjoy.

Stunning Orangy Seashells Candle

Ingredients:

- 3 drops of orange essential oil
- 5 drops of cedarwood essential oil
- 1 drop of Ylang-ylang
- Orange dye
- Seashells
- Tall dipping vat
- Metal Spoon
- Mold sealer
- Mold release
- Double boiler
- Metal Pouring Pot
- Kitchen scale
- Mold-blend wax
- Thermometer
- Small tin container
- Mold: tall triangle pillar
- Primed wick, square braided
- String

Directions:

1. Melt the wax in a double broiler then using a mold release; coat slightly the inside of candle mold.
2. Cut the wick to the appropriate length and thread it into the hole in the bottom of the mold and secure it.
3. Pour the melted wax in a metal pouring pot and stir into it right away the cedar wood with orange and Ylang-ylang essential oils followed by the orange dye then fill 90 % of the mold with it and pour the excess wax into a tin container.

4. Allow the wax to sit then re-melt the excess wax and fill with it the indentation before leaving it to sit again.
5. Tip the mold upside down to remove the candle then wrap with the string in a spiral motion starting from the bottom toward the top then secure it with some melted wax.
6. Press the seashells to the tops of the candle by using some melted wax.
7. Pour the melted wax into a dipping vat then hold the candle by its wick on top and dip it into it before allowing to set then trim top and bottom wick.

Lovely Sage Calm Candle

Ingredients:

- 3 drops of clary sage essential oil
- 6 drops of grapefruit essential oil
- 3 drops of cedar wood essential oil
- Brow, green and ivory dyes
- 3 small tin containers
- Mold sealer
- Mold release
- Double boiler
- Metal Pouring Pot
- Kitchen scale
- Mold-blend wax
- Thermometer
- Small tin container
- Mold: tall triangle pillar
- Metal skewer
- Primed wick, square braided
- Scissors

Directions:

1. Melt the wax in a double broiler then using a mold release; coat slightly the inside of candle mold.
2. Cut the wick to the appropriate length and thread it into the hole in the bottom of the mold and secure it.
3. Pour 1/3 of melted wax in a metal pot then stir into it dew drops of the green dye with 1/3 of the essential oils blend and pour it into the mold and allow it to set.
4. Pour half of the rest of melted wax into a metal pot and stir into it the brown dye with half of the rest of the essential oils

then pour it in the mold to on the green wax and allow it to set.

5. Repeat the process with the rest of the ingredients this time with the ivory dye then pour it on the green wax to fill the mold.

6. Tip the mold upside down to remove the candle then trim the excess wick from the top and bottom of the candle before using it and enjoy.

Gorgeous Lemony Rise Candle

Ingredients:

- 2 drops of lemongrass essential oil
- 1 drop of citronella essential oil
- 2 drops of lavender essential oil
- Bay leaves
- Incented pillar candle (3*6)
- Urn planter
- Waxed paper
- Taper-blend wax
- Dipping vat
- Double boiler
- Brown dye
- Glue pen with sponge applicator
- Kitchen scale
- Sage-green ribbon
- Thermometer

Directions:

1. Apply the glue to the back of the bay leaves then stick them to the pillar candle and set it aside to dry.
2. Lighten the pillar candle and let it burn until a pool of wax gather on top of it then pierce it small deep holes and pour in them the blend of the essential oils.
3. Melt the wax in a double broiler then pour it into the dipping vat and stir into it the brown dye.
4. Hold the candle by the wick then dip it into the melted wax, pull it and dip it another 2 times then place it on the waxed paper to sit and dry.

5. Once the candle dries, wrap the ribbon around it then place in the urn and enjoy.

Adorable Gingery Lavender Candle

Ingredients:

- 2 drops of ginger essential oil
- 1 drop of Neroli essential oil
- 2 drops of lavender essential oil
- White dye
- Dry lavender
- Mold: tea light
- Mold sealer
- Double boiler
- Metal Pouring Pot
- Kitchen scale
- Mold-blend wax
- Thermometer
- Primed wick, square braided
- Scissors

Directions:

1. Melt the wax in a double broiler then using a mold release; coat slightly the inside of candle mold.
2. Cut the wick to the appropriate length and thread it into the hole in the bottom of the mold and secure it.
3. Pour the melted wax in a metal pouring pot and stir into it right away the essential oils with dye then stir in the dry lavender.
4. Pour the wax into the molds and allow it to set up.
5. Tip the mold upside down to remove the candle then trim the excess wick from the top and bottom of the candle before using it and enjoy.

Beautiful Peppermint Calm Candle

Ingredients:

- 4 drops of peppermint essential oil
- 3 drops of rosemary essential oil
- 2 drops of lavender essential oil
- Light green wax chunks
- Double boiler
- Kitchen scale
- Mold blend wax
- Small tin container
- Thermometer
- Scissors
- Metal pouring pot
- Metal skewer
- Mold: round pillar
- Mold sealer
- Mold release
- Primed wick: square braided
- Small tin container

Directions:

1. Melt the wax in a double broiler then using a mold release; coat slightly the inside of candle mold.
2. Cut the wick to the appropriate length and thread it into the hole in the bottom of the mold and secure it then position the green chunks in the mold as you prefer.
3. Pour the melted wax in a metal pouring pot and stir into it right away the essential oils then fill 90 % of the mold with it and pour the excess wax into a tin container.

4. Allow the wax to sit then re-melt the excess wax and fill with it the indentation before leaving it to sit again.
5. Tip the mold upside down to remove the candle then trim the excess wick from the top and bottom of the candle before using it and enjoy.

Charming Dark Woods Candle

Ingredients:

- 6 drops of juniper berry essential oil
- Green and purple dye
- 2 small metal container
- Mold sealer
- Mold release
- Double boiler
- Metal Pouring Pot
- Kitchen scale
- Mold-blend wax
- Thermometer
- Small tin container
- Mold: round pillar
- Metal skewer
- Primed wick, square braided
- Scissors

Directions:

1. Melt the wax in a double broiler then using a mold release; coat slightly the inside of candle mold.
2. Cut the wick to the appropriate length and thread it into the hole in the bottom of the mold and secure it.
3. Pour 2/3 of the melted wax in a metal pouring pot and stir into it right away 2/3 of essential oils with the purple dye then pour it into the mold.
4. Poor the rest of the melted wax into a metal pot and stir into it the green dye with essential oils then pour it into the mold to fill the indentation and let it set.

5. Tip the mold upside down to remove the candle then trim the excess wick from the top and bottom of the candle before using it and enjoy.

Mysterious Into the Woods Candle

Ingredients:

- 2 drops of spruce
- 2 drops of cypress
- 1 drop of ginger
- Green and purple dye
- Medium sized pine cons
- Metal slotted spoon
- Waxed paper
- Dipping pot
- Double boiler
- Kitchen scale
- Taper blend wax
- thermometer

Directions:

1. Melt the wax in a double boiler then pour it in a dipping pot and stir into it the dye followed by the essential oils.
2. Dip the pine cones by using a slotted spoon into the wax then place them on wax paper to set.
3. Use them to lighten the fireplace for an amazing aroma.

Wonderful Fruity Light Candle

Ingredients:

- 3 drops of lemon essential oil
- 1 drop of lemongrass essential oil
- 1 drop of lavender essential oil
- Yellow wax chunks
- Mold sealer
- Mold blend wax
- Metal pouring pot
- Metal skewer
- Double boiler
- Fruit beads
- Mold: 3*diameter round pillar
- Mold release
- Primed wick: square braided
- Thermometer
- Scissors

Directions:

1. Melt the wax in a double broiler then using a mold release; coat slightly the inside of candle mold.
2. Cut the wick to the appropriate length and thread it into the hole in the bottom of the mold and secure it then position the green chunks in the mold as you prefer.
3. Pour the melted wax in a metal pouring pot and stir into it right away the essential oils then pour it into the mold on the chunks until only 90 % is full.
4. Add the rest of the chunks on top of the wax in the mold then tip the mold and remove the candle.

5. Trim the excess wick from the top and bottom of the candle before using it and enjoy.

Magnificent Berries Dream Candle

Ingredients:

- Bayberry wax
- Mold release
- Mold sealer
- Small tin container
- Scissors
- Thermometer
- Double broiler
- Kitchen scale
- Metal skewer
- Mold: 1 ½ *10 stick
- Prime wick: square braided

Directions:

1. Melt the wax in a double broiler then using a mold release; coat slightly the inside of candle mold.
2. Cut the wick to the appropriate length and thread it into the hole in the bottom of the mold and secure it.
3. Pour the melted wax in a metal pouring pot and then fill 90 % of the mold with it and pour the excess wax into a tin container.
4. Allow the wax to sit then re-melt the excess wax and fill with it the indentation before leaving it to sit again.
5. Tip the mold upside down to remove the candle then trim the excess wick from the top and bottom of the candle before using it and enjoy.

Seductive Valentine's Day Candle

Ingredients:

- 2 drops of jasmine essential oil
- 1 drop of Ylang-ylang essential oil
- 1 drop of rose essential oil
- Craft craving tool
- Dye red
- Mold sealer
- Mold release
- Double boiler
- Metal Pouring Pot
- Kitchen scale
- Mold-blend wax
- Thermometer
- Small tin container
- Mold: small round pillar
- Metal skewer
- Primed wick, square braided
- Scissors

Directions:

1. Place the mold in the freezer for 30 min.
2. Melt the wax in a double broiler then using a mold release; coat slightly the inside of candle mold.
3. Cut the wick to the appropriate length and thread it into the hole in the bottom of the mold and secure it.
4. Pour the melted wax in a metal pouring pot and stir into it right away the essential oils with red dye then fill 90 % of the mold with it and pour the excess wax into a tin container.
5. Allow the wax to sit then re-melt the excess wax and fill with it the indentation before leaving it to sit again.

6. Trim the excess wick from the top and bottom of the candle then use the carving tool to carve hearts on the candle.

Precious Sun Rise Candle

Ingredients:

- 3 drops of clove essential oil
- 4 drops of orange essential oil
- 5 drops of vanilla essential oil
- Dry orange slices
- Assorted dry foliage
- Gold dye
- Pepper berries
- Unscented white round pillar candle
- Mold sealer
- Mold release
- Double boiler
- Metal Pouring Pot
- Kitchen scale
- Mold-blend wax
- Thermometer
- Small tin container
- Mold: round pillar
- Metal skewer
- Primed wick, square braided
- Scissors

Directions:

1. Melt the wax in a double broiler then using a mold release; coat slightly the inside of candle mold.
2. Lighten the unscented white candle and let it burn until a pool of wax gather on top of it then pierce in it small deep holes and blend of essentials and place the candle in the middle of the mold.
3. Arrange the dry oranges with foliage and pepper berries in the mold.

4. Pour the melted wax in a metal pouring pot and stir into it right away the gold dye then fill 90 % of the mold with it and pour the excess wax into a tin container.
5. Use a dowel to arrange the botanicals to your liking after pouring on them the wax.
6. Allow the wax to sit then re-melt the excess wax and fill with it the indentation before leaving it to sit again.
7. Tip the mold upside down to remove the candle and enjoy.

Delightful Epic Pine Candle

Ingredients:

- 1 drop of pine essential oil
- 1 drop of spruce essential oil
- 1 drop of orange essential oil
- Burgundy dye
- Mold sealer
- Mold release
- Double boiler
- Metal Pouring Pot
- Kitchen scale
- Mold-blend wax
- Thermometer
- Small tin container
- Mold: round pillar
- Metal skewer
- Primed wick, square braided
- Scissors

Directions:

1. Place the mold in the freezer for 30 min.
2. Melt the wax in a double broiler then using a mold release; coat slightly the inside of candle mold.
3. Cut the wick to the appropriate length and thread it into the hole in the bottom of the mold and secure it.
4. Pour the melted wax in a metal pouring pot and stir into it right away the essential oils with burgundy dye then fill 90 % of the mold with it and pour the excess wax into a tin container.

5. Allow the wax to sit then re-melt the excess wax and fill with it the indentation before leaving it to sit again.
6. Trim the excess wick from the top and bottom of the candle then use it and enjoy.

Pleasurable Lovers Night Candle

Ingredients:

- 4 drops of cedar wood essential oil
- 3 drops of orange essential oil
- 1 drop of clove essential oil
- 1 drop of cinnamon essential oil
- Red dye
- Hair dryer
- Mold sealer
- Mold release
- Double boiler
- Metal Pouring Pot
- Kitchen scale
- Mold-blend wax
- Thermometer
- Small tin container
- Mold: 4 diameter round pillar
- Spatula
- Metal skewer
- Primed wick, square braided
- Scissors
- Metal fork

Directions:

1. Melt the wax in a double broiler then using a mold release; coat slightly the inside of candle mold.
2. Cut the wick to the appropriate length and thread it into the hole in the bottom of the mold and secure it.
3. Pour the melted wax in a metal pouring pot and stir into it right away the essential oils with burgundy dye then fill 90 % of the mold with it and pour the excess wax into a tin container while reserving some wax for later use.

4. Allow the wax to sit then re-melt the excess wax and fill with it the indentation before leaving it to sit again.
5. Trim the excess wick from the top and bottom of the candle.
6. Using a fork, whip the rest of the melted wax until it becomes thick and foamy for 5 to 10 min.
7. Warm the sides of the candle with a hair dryer then use a spatula to apply a thick coat of the wax to cover the entire candle.
8. Set the candle to dry then use it and enjoy.

Refreshing Lemon Stars Candle

Ingredients:

- 3 drops of lemongrass essential oil
- 2 drops of lavender essential oil
- White dye
- cookie sheet
- Craft knife
- Double boiler
- Kitchen scale
- Metal pouring pot
- Metal skewer
- Mold release
- Mold sealer
- Mold-blend wax
- Primed wick: paper or metal core
- Scissors
- Small tin container
- Spatula
- Star cookie cutter
- Thermometer
- Wick tab
- Wicking needle

Directions:

1. Melt the wax in a double broiler then using a mold release; coat slightly the inside of ¼ inch cooking sheet.
2. Pour the melted wax in a metal pouring pot and stir into it right away the essential oils with white dye then pour it into the cookie sheet.
3. While the wax is still warm, cut it with a star cookie cutter and pierce the middle of each star with wicking needle a hole then let it sit.

4. One the wax sit, remove the stars with a spatula.
5. Attach 12 inches of wick to a wick tab then thread its unattached end to a wicking needle then thread the stars into it.
6. Trim the wick on top then use it and enjoy.

Incredible Glassy Lamp Bottle Candle

Ingredients:

- 5 drops of lavender essential oil
- 4 drops of eucalyptus essential oil
- 2 drops of lemon essential oil
- Floral wire
- Wire cutters
- Clear lamp oil
- Clear and tall decorative bottle
- Eucalyptus branches
- Glass tube with wick

Directions:

1. Arrange the eucalyptus branches inside the decorative bottle and use the floral wire to secure them then place the tube with wick in inside the bottle and wire it to the branches to keep it in place.
2. Add the essential oils to the lamp oil the pour it in the glass bottle.
3. Use your lamp bottle and enjoy.

Enchanting Soothing Rosemary Candle

Ingredients:

- 6 drops of thyme
- double boiler
- Yellow and red dyes
- Kitchen scale
- Metal pouring pot
- Metal skewer
- Mold: round pillar
- Mold release
- Mold sealer
- Mold-blend wax
- Primed wick: square-braided
- Scissors
- 2 small metal containers
- 1 small tin container
- Thermometer

Directions:

1. Melt the wax in a double broiler then using a mold release; coat slightly the inside of candle mold.
2. Cut the wick to the appropriate length and thread it into the hole in the bottom of the mold and secure it.
3. Pour 2/3 of the melted wax in a metal pouring pot and stir into it right away 2/3 of essential oils blend with the red dye then pour it into the mold.
4. Poor the rest of the melted wax into a metal pot and stir into it the yellow dye with essential oils then pour it into the mold to fill the indentation and let it set.
5. Tip the mold upside down to remove the candle then trim the excess wick from the top and bottom of the candle before using it and enjoy.

Stunning Rosemary Fantasy Candle

Ingredients:

- 1 drop of geranium essential oil
- 1 drop of rosemary essential oil
- 1 drop of juniper essential oil
- double boiler
- Green Dye
- Rosemary
- Mold: square
- Mold release
- Mold sealer
- Mold-blend wax
- Primed wick: square braided
- Scissors
- Thermometer
- Kitchen scale
- Metal fork
- 2 metal pouring pots
- Metal skewer

Directions:

1. Melt the wax in a double broiler then using a mold release; coat slightly the inside of candle mold.
2. Cut the wick to the appropriate length and thread it into the hole in the bottom of the mold and secure it.
3. Divide the melted wax into 2 and pour them into 2 metal pouring pots then place the bottom part of 1 pot in a double boiler to keep the wax melt and allow the wax in the other one to cool down until a light film forms.
4. Whip the cold wax with a fork until it becomes foamy and light in color then pull the 2 waxes into the mold.
5. Tip the mold upside down to remove the candle then trim the excess wick from the top and bottom of the candle before using it and enjoy.

Elegant Heavenly Geranium Candle

Ingredients:

- 4 drops of geranium essential oil
- 2 drops of bergamot essential oil
- 1 drop of lavender essential oil
- Dipping vat
- Double boiler
- Pressed flowers
- Thermometer
- White round and unscented pillar candle
- Waxed paper
- Glue pen
- Kitchen scale
- Metal pouring pot
- Paraffin wax

Directions:

1. Melt the wax in a double broiler then using a mold release; coat slightly the inside of candle mold.
2. Lighten the unscented white candle and let it burn until a pool of wax gather on top of it then pierce in it small deep holes and blend of essentials and place the kindle in the middle of the mold.
3. Attach the pressed flowers to the pillar candle by using the glue pen.
4. Pour the wax into the dipping pot and dip in it the flower candle while holding it by the wick.
5. Press down any flowers that getting detached then place the candle on the waxed paper and let it sit.

Marvelous Royal Cajeput Candle

Ingredients:

- 5 drops of Cajeput essential oil
- 2 drops of lavender
- beige ribbon
- Drill and drill bit in the size of a glass vial
- Dry flowers
- Glass vial with wick tubing
- Lamp oil
- Sage-green unscented pillar candle 2*10

Directions:

1. Drill carefully and quickly a hole in the unscented pillar candle to accommodate the length of the glass vial.
2. Place the glass vial inside the candle then mix the essential oils with lamp oil and pour it into it to fill only 90 % of it.
3. Insert the wick with tubing into the glass vial then tie flowers to the candle and use it.

Super Rosy Bliss Candle

Ingredients:

- 3 drops of rose essential oil
- 2 drops of lavender essential oil
- 2 drops of orange essential oil
- Red dye
- double boiler
- kitchen scale
- metal pouring pot
- scissors
- small tin container
- snowflake or mineral oil
- thermometer
- metal skewer
- mold: large heart
- mold re lease
- mold sealer
- mold-blend wax
- primed wick: square-braided

Directions:

1. Melt the wax in a double broiler then using a mold release; coat slightly the inside of candle mold.
2. Cut the wick to the appropriate length and thread it into the hole in the bottom of the mold and secure it then add the snowflake oil according to directions of the manufacturer.
3. Pour the melted wax in a metal pouring pot and stir into it right away the essential oils with dye then fill 90 % of the mold with it and pour the excess wax into a tin container.
4. Allow the wax to sit then re-melt the excess wax and fill with it the indentation before leaving it to sit again.
5. Tip the mold upside down to remove the candle then trim the excess wick from the top and bottom of the candle before using it and enjoy.

Delicate Classy Roses Candle

Ingredients:

- 3 drops of petit grain essential oil
- 1 drop of cedar wood
- 1 drop of 1 drop of rosemary essential oil
- Beach glass
- Seashells: including sea horses and starfish....
- rosemary
- Glass tube with wick
- Wire cutters
- Clear lamp oil
- Clear decorative jar

Directions:

1. Arrange the seashells with beach glass in the decorative jar as you prefer.
2. Insert the glass tube with wick in the jar then blend the essential oils with lamp oil and add it into the jar.
3. Light your oil lamp and enjoy.

The Charming Golden Age Candle

Ingredients:

- 13 drops of mandarin orange essential oil
- 7 drops of neroli essential oil
- 5 drops of clary sage essential oil
- Orange dye
- Black aquarium rocks
- Corrugated cardboard
- Mold sealer
- Mold: tall triangular
- Mold -blend wax
- Primed wick: square-braided
- Scissors
- Small tin container
- Vegetable oil spray
- Thermometer
- Double boiler
- Hair pins
- Kitchen scale
- Metal pouring pot
- Metal skewer
- Mold release

Directions:

1. Melt the wax in a double broiler then using a mold release; coat slightly the inside of candle mold.
2. Cut the corrugated cardboard to fit inside the mold then spray with vegetable oil spray and place it in the mold with corrugated side in the mold.
3. Secure it by against the edges of the mold by placing the hair pins the its center and over the outside of the mold.
4. Cut the wick to the appropriate length and thread it into the hole in the bottom of the mold and secure it then place the

black aquarium rocks in the bottom of the mold (1 to 2 inches).

5. Pour the melted wax in a metal pouring pot and stir into it right away the essential oils with dye then fill 90 % of the mold with it and pour the excess wax into a tin container.
6. Allow the wax to sit then re-melt the excess wax and fill with it the indentation before leaving it to sit again.
7. Tip the mold upside down to remove the candle then trim the excess wick from the top and bottom of the candle and remove the cardboard before using it and enjoy.

Divine Sunny Light Candle

Ingredients:

- 2 drops of cedar wood essential oil
- 2 drops of vetiver essential oil
- Double boiler
- Orange dye
- Kitchen scale
- Small tin container
- Thermometer
- Wicks: paper or wire core
- 5 Wick tabs
- Metal pouring pot
- 3 molds: square votives
- Mold release
- Mold sealer
- Mold-blend wax (enough to make 3)
- Scissors

Directions:

1. Melt the wax in a double broiler then using a mold release; coat slightly the inside of candle mold.
2. Cut the wick to the appropriate length and secure it to a wick tab then repeat the process with left wick tabs.
6. Pour 2/3 of the melted wax in a metal pouring pot and stir into it right away 2 drops of cedar wood and vetiver essential oils blend with the orange dye then pour it into the mold and pour the excess wax into a tin container.
7. Allow the wax to sit then re-melt the excess wax and fill with it the indentation before leaving it to sit again.
3. Poor the rest of the melted wax into a metal pot and stir into it the yellow dye with essential oils then pour it into the mold to fill the indentation and let it set.

4. Tip the mold upside down to remove the candle then trim the excess wick from the top and bottom of the candle before using it and enjoy.

Conclusion

Thank you again for downloading this book! I really do hope you found the recipes as tasty and mouth watering as I did.

Printed in Great Britain
by Amazon